ECO crafts

CREATE WITH CARDBOARD

written by
Marcy Morin
and **Heidi E. Thompson**

CAPSTONE PRESS
a capstone imprint

Dabble Lab is published by Capstone Press, an imprint of Capstone.
1710 Roe Crest Drive
North Mankato, Minnesota 56003
capstonepub.com

Library of Congress Cataloging-in-Publication Data is available on the Library of Congress website.
ISBN: 978-1-4966-9590-1 (hardcover)
ISBN: 978-1-6639-0731-8 (ebook PDF)

Summary: What can you make with a box? Anything you can imagine! A way-cool cellphone holder, a party piñata, savvy storage solutions, and more! Think outside the box with more than 10 easy recycled cardboard projects!

Image Credits
Mighty Media, Inc. (project photos): Front Cover, Back Cover, 3, 4, 6, 7, 8, 9, 10, 11, 12, 13, 14, 15, 16, 17, 18, 19, 20, 21, 22, 23, 24, 25, 26, 27, 28, 29, 30, 31

Design Elements: Shutterstock Images: Alina Kholopova, Arina P Habich, donatas1205, Elena Polovinko, I WALL, Lizard, Lu Vesper, Madiz, Maglara, SHTRAUS DMYTRO, Vera Aksionava, xpixel

Editorial and Design Credits
Editor: Rebecca Felix, Mighty Media; Designer: Aruna Rangarajan, Mighty Media

All internet sites appearing in back matter were available and accurate when this book was sent to press.

For my Mama, for teaching me all things crafty!
—MM

For Bray, Cole, and Isaac, who keep me creative and on my toes. —HT

TABLE OF CONTENTS

Cardboard Is Everywhere! 4

Party Piñata Monster 6

Mosaic Pet Portrait 8

Desktop Organizer 10

Leaf Ornaments................................. 12

Bee Sanctuary 14

Paperboard Planets 16

Whale Phone Holder.......................... 18

Goat Puppet 20

Cardboard Cactus.............................. 24

Mountain Wall Art 26

Egg Carton Wind Chimes 30

Read More 32

Internet Sites...................................... 32

CARDBOARD IS EVERYWHERE!

Many everyday items come packaged in it, from cereal to shoes. When we're done with cardboard, we recycle it. But with creativity, you can turn used cardboard into new items!

WITH CARDBOARD, THERE'S NO LIMIT TO WHAT YOU CAN CREATE.

Upcycle all types of cardboard into eco crafts. Maybe you'll make a **colorful piñata**. You could create a cool **cell phone holder**. You might even build a **bee sanctuary** to hang from a tree!

NOW, GATHER SOME CARDBOARD AND GET READY TO CRAFT!

The crafts in this book use materials you'll likely find at home. Come across something you can't find? Think of ways to adapt the project using items you do have.

AND BE SURE TO ASK FOR AN ADULT'S HELP WITH ANY SHARP TOOLS OR OBJECTS.

PARTY PIÑATA MONSTER

WHAT'S BETTER THAN A PARTY? A PARTY **WITH A PIÑATA!** TRANSFORM AN EMPTY TISSUE BOX INTO A CANDY CONTAINER. THEN FIND A BAT AND HAVE A BLAST!

WHAT YOU NEED

- ribbon
- ruler
- scissors
- pencil
- empty tissue box
- crepe paper
- craft glue
- foam brush
- candy
- googly eyes or paper and markers

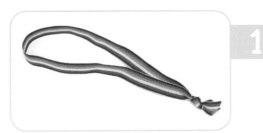

1 Cut a 24-inch (61-centimeter) piece of ribbon. Fold it in half. Then knot the loose ends.

2 Use the pencil to poke a small hole in a top corner of the box. Thread the ribbon's loop through the poked hole from inside the box.

ECO FACTS

Facial tissues are made from paper pulp. Americans wipe their noses with billions of disposable tissues every year.

WHAT TO DO

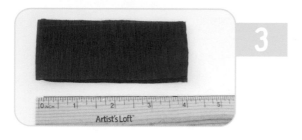

3

Cut a long strip of crepe paper. Fold the strip on top of itself into small sections. Make each about 4 inches (10 cm) wide.

4

Cut small slits halfway up the folded crepe paper. Unfold the strip.

5

Brush a line of glue around the sides of the box, starting at the bottom. Wrap the strip of crepe paper around the box.

6

Repeat steps 3 through 5 to cover the sides of the box. Then cover the bottom of the box with layers of more cut crepe paper.

7

Fill the box with candy through its top opening. Then cover the top of the box with more cut crepe paper.

• FINAL STEP!

GLUE EYES ON YOUR PIÑATA TO MAKE IT A GOOFY MONSTER!

MOSAIC PET PORTRAIT

LOOKING FOR A PET PROJECT? THIS CRAFT IS A GEOMETRIC WORK OF ART. MAKE A MOSAIC MASTERPIECE OF YOUR FAVORITE ANIMAL!

WHAT YOU NEED

- paperboard (cereal or cracker boxes)
- scissors
- pencil
- paint and paintbrush
- craft glue
- corrugated cardboard box

WHAT TO DO

1 Cut one large side from the paperboard to make a flat sheet. Draw the outline of your favorite pet on the sheet.

2 Cut out the shape.

8

3 Paint the shape one color.

4 Cut shapes from extra paperboard to create your animal's features. This could include ears, eyes, a nose or beak, or scales. Paint the shapes other colors and glue them to your pet cutout.

5 Ask an adult to cut a square of the corrugated cardboard. This will be a mount for your pet mosaic. Paint the cardboard and let it dry.

FINAL STEP!

GLUE YOUR PET PORTRAIT TO THE CARDBOARD AND DISPLAY IT!!

DESKTOP ORGANIZER

DO YOU HAVE A MESSY DESK? MAKE A **STACKABLE ORGANIZER** OUT OF A FEW SUPPLIES. THIS CRAFT WILL HELP UNCLUTTER YOUR DESK. AND IT'LL KEEP CARDBOARD CLUTTER FROM ENDING UP IN A LANDFILL!

WHAT YOU NEED

- shoebox
- scissors
- pencil
- ruler
- craft knife
- colorful duct tape
- hot glue and hot glue gun

1 Open the shoebox up at its seams. Cut along the folds to make several cardboard pieces.

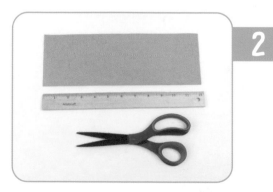

2 Measure and cut a 12-by-4-inch (30.5-by-10-cm) strip.

3 Measure and mark three equal sections, each 4 inches (10 cm) in length. Ask an adult to use a craft knife to score the lines you drew. This will make the cardboard easier to fold.

4 Fold the cardboard at the marks to make a triangle. Unfold the triangle for the next step.

5 Cover both sides of the cardboard in duct tape. Then shape it back into a triangle. Use more tape to connect the ends.

6 Repeat steps 2 to 5 to make multiple triangles.

• FINAL STEP!

STACK AND GLUE THE TRIANGLES TOGETHER TO CREATE YOUR DESKTOP ORGANIZER!

LEAF ORNAMENTS

RECREATE NATURE'S BEAUTY INDOORS! REPURPOSE PAPERBOARD AND MAGAZINE PAGES TO MAKE **COLORFUL LEAVES**. THEN HANG THEM IN YOUR HOME.

WHAT YOU NEED

- magazine pages
- hole punch
- pencil
- paperboard (cereal or cracker boxes)
- scissors
- craft glue
- paintbrush
- pushpin
- string

WHAT TO DO

1 Use the hole punch to create piles of confetti out of magazine pages.

2 Cut along the paperboard box seams to create a flat sheet. Draw leaf shapes on the sheet. Cut out the shapes. Draw veins on the leaves if you like. These will peek through the confetti.

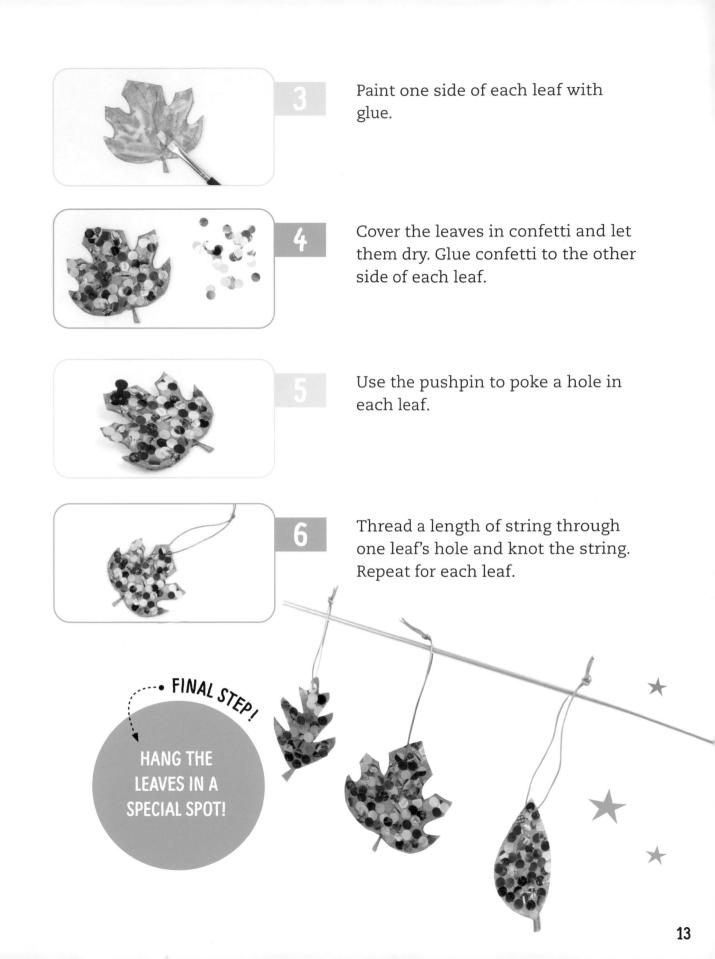

3 Paint one side of each leaf with glue.

4 Cover the leaves in confetti and let them dry. Glue confetti to the other side of each leaf.

5 Use the pushpin to poke a hole in each leaf.

6 Thread a length of string through one leaf's hole and knot the string. Repeat for each leaf.

FINAL STEP!

HANG THE LEAVES IN A SPECIAL SPOT!

✳ BEE ✳ SANCTUARY

BEES ARE NATURE'S GARDENERS. THEY POLLINATE DIFFERENT PLANTS, HELPING TO FORM FRUITS, VEGETABLES, AND EVEN NEW SEEDS. WITHOUT BEES, WE WOULD BE WITHOUT MANY FOODS! REUSE EVERYDAY ITEMS TO CREATE A **SAFE PLACE FOR BEES TO NEST**.

WHAT YOU NEED

- tall, narrow cardboard box (or paperboard milk carton)
- scissors
- paint and paintbrushes
- clear packing tape
- pencil
- twine
- cardboard tubes
- paper straws
- sticks and twigs

WHAT TO DO

1

Remove the lid or cut the top flaps off the box. Paint the box and let it dry.

2

Wrap clear packing tape around the outside of the box. This will help protect it from rain.

ECO FACTS

Your bee sanctuary will attract cavity-nesting bees. This type of wild bee lays eggs in plant stems and holes in wood. These bees are great pollinators for your garden!

3 Lay the box on one long side. Use the pencil to punch a hole near the box's open end. Punch another hole near its closed end.

4 Cut a piece of twine. Make it long enough to thread through the punched holes and create two long tails outside the box. Thread the twine through the holes from inside the box.

5 Cut a cardboard tube in half the long way. Roll up each half the long way to create two long, thin cylinders. Tape each cylinder together to secure. Repeat this step to make several more cylinders.

6 Trim the cylinders, paper straws, and sticks. Make them a little shorter than the length of the box.

7 Pack the box tightly with the straws, sticks, and cylinders.

• FINAL STEP!

TIE YOUR BEE SANCTUARY SNUGLY TO A TREE BRANCH FACING SOUTH OR SOUTHEAST.

PAPERBOARD PLANETS

TURN YOUR EMPTY CEREAL BOXES INTO **SPACE ART!** COLORFUL STRIPS TRANSFORM INTO SPINNING PLANETS IN THIS FUN CRAFT.

WHAT YOU NEED

- paperboard (cereal or cracker boxes)
- scissors
- paint and paintbrush
- ruler
- pencil
- pushpin
- brads (metal fasteners)
- oil pastels
- yarn

WHAT TO DO

1 Unfold a cereal box. Cut off the flaps. Then cut along one seam. This creates a large, flat sheet of paperboard.

2 Paint each side of the paperboard a different color. Let it dry.

ECO FACTS

A cereal box can be recycled and turned into a new cereal box up to six times. After that, the cardboard's fiber becomes too weak to reuse.

3 Across the paperboard's length, measure and cut out strips that are 1 inch (2.5 cm) wide.

4 Use the pushpin to make a hole about ½ inch (1.3 cm) from each end of each strip. Widen the holes slightly using the tip of the pencil.

5 Stack the strips. Push a brad through their holes on one end. Open the brad to secure it. Secure the other ends of the strips with another brad.

6 Slowly spread the strips out to create a sphere. Decorate the outside of your orb! Use oil pastels to make planetary swirls, rings, and more.

7 Thread a piece a yarn through the top of the sphere. Tie the ends in a knot to make a hanger.

•·· **FINAL STEP!**

TRY MAKING MORE SPHERES USING DIFFERENT NUMBERS AND LENGTHS OF STRIPS!

WHALE PHONE HOLDER

DOES YOUR PHONE NEED A NICE PLACE TO REST OVERNIGHT? CRAFT A COLORFUL VESSEL TO KEEP IT SAFE ON THE SEAS (OR JUST YOUR NIGHTSTAND!). CARDBOARD BECOMES A CUTE WHALE IN A FEW EASY STEPS.

WHAT YOU NEED

- pencil
- corrugated cardboard
- utility knife or scissors
- ruler
- hot glue and hot glue gun
- paint and paintbrush
- markers or gems

WHAT TO DO

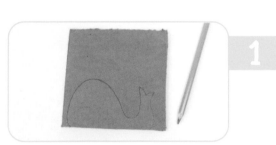

1 Sketch a whale on cardboard. Make the whale about the size of your cell phone.

2 Have an adult cut out your whale shape.

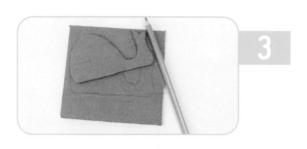

3

Trace the cutout on another cardboard square. Then have an adult cut out the traced shape as well.

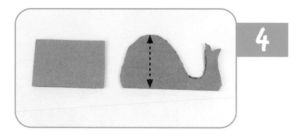

4

Measure the height of the whale's head. Have an adult cut out a cardboard rectangle that is the whale's height by 3 inches (8 cm). This will be the first connecting piece.

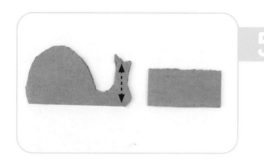

5

Measure the height of the whale's tail. Have an adult cut out a cardboard rectangle that is the tail's height by 3 inches (8 cm). This is the second connecting piece.

6

Glue the connecting pieces to your whale so the 3-inch sides are horizontal. This creates the space where your phone will rest.

FINAL STEP!

PAINT THE WHALE AND DECORATE IT USING MARKERS OR GEMS!

GOAT PUPPET

DO YOU HAVE USED CARDBOARD TUBES IN YOUR HOUSE? SAVE THEM FROM THE RECYCLING BIN AND BUILD A **PRANCING PUPPET**. ONCE YOU HAVE ONE DONE, MAKE MORE ANIMALS!

WHAT YOU NEED

- 2 cardboard tubes
- scissors
- paint and paintbrush
- 2 craft sticks
- string
- pushpin
- toothpick
- ruler
- marker
- pipe cleaner (chenille stem)
- tape

1 Leave one tube whole for your goat's body. Cut off one-third of the other tube. The larger piece of that will be your goat's head.

2 Paint all three tube pieces inside and out. Let them dry.

20

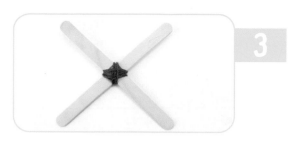

3 Make an X with the craft sticks. Wrap a length of cut string around the point where the sticks cross. Tie the string to secure the sticks.

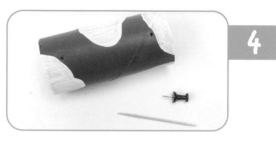

4 Use the pushpin to poke two parallel holes into the body tube. Make one hole at each end along the top of the body. Slightly widen the holes with a toothpick.

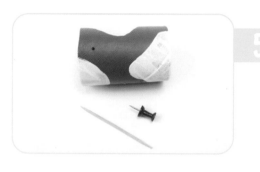

5 At one end of the head tube, poke a hole ½ inch (1.3 cm) from the end. Poke a second hole across from the first on the same end of the tube. Make the second hole 1 inch (2.5 cm) in from the end.

6 Cut two 12-inch (30.5-cm) pieces of string. Tie a knot at one end of each. Then, from inside the tube, thread each unknotted end through one hole in the body tube.

7 In one string, tie a knot where you want the head to rest. Then thread the unknotted end of that string up through the holes in the head tube. Start with the hole that is farther in from the end of the head tube.

Project continued on the next page

8 Grab the X from step 3. Tie the end of each string to opposite ends of the same craft stick.

9 Cut out horns from the remaining cardboard tube. Glue the horns to the head.

10 Draw eyes with the marker.

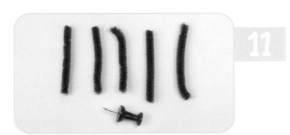

11 Cut the pipe cleaner into five equal pieces. Use the pushpin to poke four small holes for legs. Make these holes in the underside of the body tube.

ECO FACTS

Shigeru Ban is a Japanese architect. He constructs temporary homes and other buildings out of cardboard tubes. Ban often builds these structures to shelter people whose homes get damaged by natural disasters.

12 Insert a pipe cleaner piece into each leg hole. Bend the pieces inside the tube to secure them in place. Bend the other ends to look like feet.

13 Tape the remaining pipe cleaner piece inside the tube as a tail.

• FINAL STEP!

HOLD AND MOVE THE CRAFT-STICK X TO MAKE YOUR PUPPET MOVE. WATCH IT PRANCE, WALK, AND CLIMB!

CARDBOARD CACTUS

PLANTS BRING LIFE TO ANY ROOM! BUT PLANTS ALSO REQUIRE CARE. IF YOU HAVE A HARD TIME REMEMBERING TO WATER, THIS **PAPER PLANT** IS PERFECT. BUILD IT AND ADMIRE IT. NO CARE NEEDED!

WHAT YOU NEED

- empty oatmeal container or other cylindrical cardboard container
- utility knife
- craft glue
- old magazine
- scissors
- markers
- stickers
- corrugated cardboard
- pencil
- paint and paintbrush
- toothpicks
- hot glue and hot glue gun
- rocks, pebbles, acorns, or other natural materials

1 Ask an adult to cut the container's height to 4 or 5 inches (10 or 13 cm). This will be your planter pot. Use craft glue to decorate it with old magazine page cutouts. Let the glue dry. Then decorate the pot with markers and stickers.

2 Draw two cactus shapes on the corrugated cardboard. Make sure the cactuses can fit inside the container from step 1. Have an adult help you cut out the shapes.

24

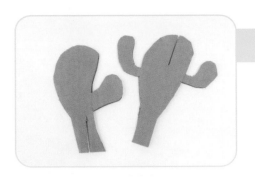

3 Starting from the base, have an adult cut a slit about one-third up the length of one cactus stem. Repeat for the second cactus, but this time cut down starting from the top.

4 Paint the front and back of each cactus and let them dry.

5 Wedge the two cactus pieces together at the slits you created in step 3.

CAREFUL!
THE CACTUS "SPINES" WILL BE SHARP.

6 Paint the toothpicks and let them dry. Then cut them into smaller pieces and hot glue these to the cactus as spines.

• FINAL STEP!

PLACE YOUR FINISHED CACTUS IN YOUR DECORATED CONTAINER. FILL AROUND THE CACTUS WITH ROCKS, ACORNS, OR OTHER NATURE ITEMS TO HOLD IT IN PLACE!

MOUNTAIN WALL ART

NATURE SHOWS OFF AWESOME LANDSCAPES DAY AND NIGHT! RECREATE A **SCENIC VIEW** WITH SOME CARDBOARD. IF YOU'D LIKE, HIDE TINY LIGHTS IN IT TO MAKE YOUR ARTWORK GLOW!

WHAT YOU NEED

- corrugated cardboard box
- utility knife or scissors
- ruler
- pencil
- paint and paintbrush
- hot glue and hot glue gun
- string of battery-powered LED lights (optional)

WHAT TO DO

1 Ask an adult to help you cut three cardboard rectangles. Make the first 12 by 8 inches (30.5 by 20 cm), the second 12 by 6 inches (30.5 by 15 cm), and the third 12 by 3 inches (30.5 by 8 cm).

2 Draw mountain peaks across the length of the two smaller rectangles. Then cut along the mountaintops.

3 Paint the mountain pieces and the rectangular backboard. Add a moon and stars. Let the paint dry.

4 Have an adult cut out 12 cardboard squares. Make six of the squares 2-by-2-inches (5-by-5-cm). Make the other six squares 1-by-1-inch (2.5-by-2.5-cm).

5 Glue the smaller squares together in three pairs. Repeat with the larger squares.

Project continued on the next page

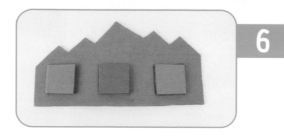

6

Glue the three larger square pairs to the back of the larger mountain piece.

7

Glue the three smaller square pairs to the back of the smaller mountain piece.

8

Line up the bottom of the larger mountain piece with the bottom of the backboard. Glue the mounted square pieces to the backboard.

9

Line up the bottom of the smaller mountain piece with the bottom of the larger mountain piece. Glue its mounted squares on top of the first set of mountains.

ECO FACTS

In the United States, more than 90 percent of shipped products are contained in corrugated boxes. This equals more than 80 billion cardboard boxes used each year!

• FINAL STEP!

HANG YOUR WALL ART. IF YOU'D LIKE, TUCK A STRING OF LED LIGHTS BEHIND THE MOUNTAINS TO ADD A STARRY GLOW!

EGG CARTON WIND CHIMES

AN EGG CARTON'S PURPOSE NEED NOT END WHEN ITS CONTENTS BECOME OMELETS! REPURPOSE A CARTON INTO A **WIND CHIME**. CREATE A CALM MOOD IN AN OUTDOOR SPACE.

WHAT YOU NEED

- yarn, string, or twine
- scissors
- stick
- egg carton
- paint and paintbrush
- toothpick
- hot glue and hot glue gun
- bells

WHAT TO DO

1 Cut a piece of yarn and tie it to each end of the stick. This creates a triangle hanger.

2 Cut each cup out of the carton.

3 Paint the cups your favorite colors inside and out. Let them dry.

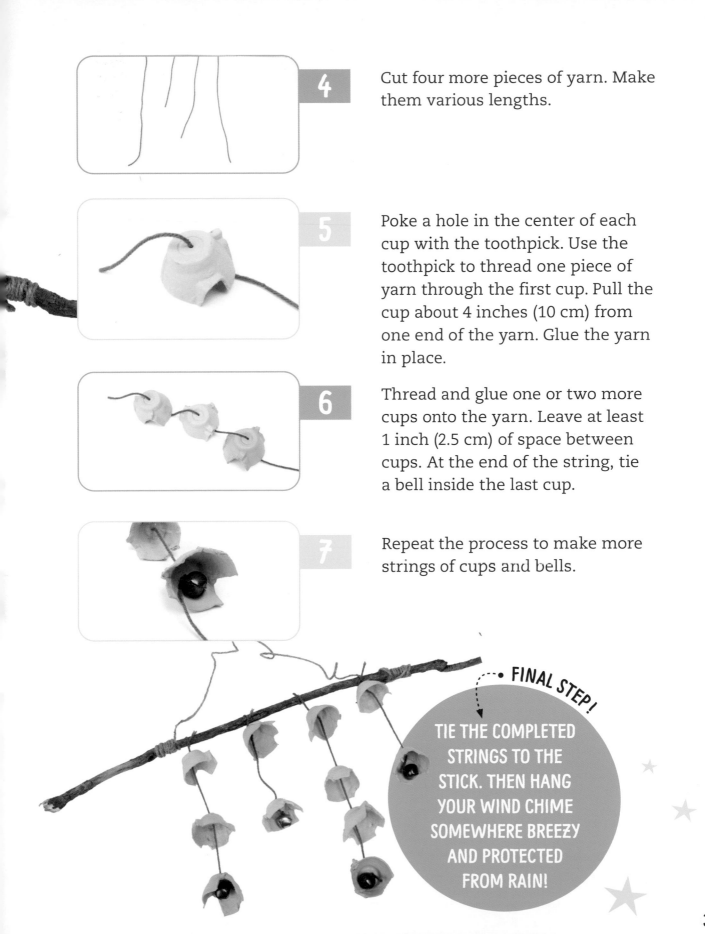

4 Cut four more pieces of yarn. Make them various lengths.

5 Poke a hole in the center of each cup with the toothpick. Use the toothpick to thread one piece of yarn through the first cup. Pull the cup about 4 inches (10 cm) from one end of the yarn. Glue the yarn in place.

6 Thread and glue one or two more cups onto the yarn. Leave at least 1 inch (2.5 cm) of space between cups. At the end of the string, tie a bell inside the last cup.

7 Repeat the process to make more strings of cups and bells.

FINAL STEP!

TIE THE COMPLETED STRINGS TO THE STICK. THEN HANG YOUR WIND CHIME SOMEWHERE BREEZY AND PROTECTED FROM RAIN!

READ MORE

Manlapig, Leslie. *Travel Through Time with Cardboard & Duct Tape.* North Mankato, MN: Capstone Press, 2018.

McLeod, Kimberly. *Fun and Easy Crafting with Recycled Materials: 60 Cool Projects that Reimagine Paper Rolls, Egg Cartons, Jars and More!* Salem, MA: Page Street Publishing Co., 2019.

Oliver, Carin. *Cat Castles: 20 Cardboard Habitats You Can Build Yourself.* Philadelphia: Quirk Books, 2016.

INTERNET SITES

*The Kid Should See This—***Community-Built Miniature Cardboard Cities** thekidshouldseethis.com/post/alfredo-and-isabel-aquilizan -cardboard-homes

*KidsHealth—***Be a Green Kid** kidshealth.org/en/kids/go-green.html

*KWD Kids Recycling—***Recycling** kwdkids.com/recycling/